DAVID WESTON
An Artist at Home and Abroad

FOR MARY

In the year of our fiftieth anniversary.
For your unswerving encouragement and loyalty,
but most of all for your love.

DAVID WESTON
An Artist at Home and Abroad

HALSGROVE

First published in Great Britain in 2007

British Library Cataloguing-in-Publication Data
A CIP record for this title is available from the British Library

ISBN 978 1 84114 611 9

HALSGROVE
Halsgrove House
Ryelands Industrial Estate
Bagley Green, Wellington
Somerset TA21 9PZ
Tel: 01823 653777
Fax: 01823 216796
email: sales@halsgrove.com
website: www.halsgrove.com

Printed and bound by D'Auria Industrie Grafiche Spa, Italy

Contents

Acknowledgements

To Simon Butler, my publisher, I owe a great debt of thanks for his agreement to publish this second collection of my paintings for Halsgrove. Both Karen Binaccioni and Denise Lyons have once again pulled out all the stops to make this book a success, and my thanks go to all the staff at Halsgrove for their enthusiasm over its production and launch.

My daughter Karen, with her usual aplomb, has deciphered my hand-written text and made good sense of what I intended to convey.

Some photographic work was done by Paul Brown Imaging and Roger Brooks of West End Gallery and my thanks go to them for their work in that direction.

A number of the paintings reproduced within these pages were borrowed from their owners for photography and I am extremely grateful to them for their willingness to put up with bare walls whilst the process was achieved.

Lastly, my unreserved appreciation must go to my wife Mary and my family for their consistent support whilst I was working on this book and which has been so much a part of my painting life during the last couple of years.

An Artist at Home and Abroad

Most days when I am at home my morning walk takes me down towards the church at the bottom of the village. Kirby Bellars, in the heart of Leicestershire's Quorn Hunt country is a pleasant mix of old and new houses, although increasingly the newer ones it seems are exceeding those from a previous century.

This is where my wife Mary and I set down our roots some thirty-seven years ago although we were both Leicestershire born and bred. I am sure my roots have influenced the way I paint and indeed the variety of subjects I enjoy tackling, and although Kirby Bellars itself has nothing spectacular to offer as English villages go, I have come to feel very much at one with the area and our own surroundings in particular, and that is very important to me as an artist. The wanderlust bug only bites a few times a year and then it doesn't take me away for very long. I have never had desires to spend prolonged periods painting abroad.

But for the moment I must keep my thoughts in Kirby Bellars. There is a lovely line of lime trees that on a sunny day filter the sunlight on the approach to the church and from there the road goes no further, but a delightful footpath takes one on to the lake that lies beyond with its Broadland style landscape and good variety of wildfowl. I feel it to be the best part of Kirby Bellars for there is always a peaceful feel to the environs of the church and its meadows in all seasons. The nearest cottage, passed on the way down, is a good one hundred yards distant, so the slight remoteness from the village gives these few acres an atmosphere that is quintessentially English.

The church dates from the thirteenth century, and just outside the porch is a rather nice seat where in spring and summer months the morning sun beckons one along the path from the iron gates to maybe sit for a while and take in the varied beauty of the surrounding trees. It is a happy place to relax for a time, or even just occasionally to reflect on the wider issues of life. Certainly it is a great place to take in the best of an English morning sun and maybe plan a little of the day ahead. As the man said, "Sometimes I sits and thinks, and sometimes I just sits," and that's about how it is for me.

Planning the day's work usually means that my mind will inevitably be back in the studio at my home at the top of the village. Perhaps a new painting will be ready to start or something is halfway complete where it has been left from a previous session whilst thought is given to its progress towards completion. Many a painting has been conceived and to some extent executed in my mind whilst enjoying that seat by the church porch. A little planning goes a long way towards the success of a painting – as most of my paintings are produced these days from sketch-book drawings done on

Interior, Kirby Bellars
Watercolour 8.5"x7.5"

location I like to choose my subject a day or two beforehand which gives time for real thought and, if one is lucky, to see the finished picture in the mind's eye before starting to paint. That mind's eye image is not always there and when it is it is only momentary, no more than a fleeting glimpse of the completed painting. This can be a trifle frustrating but nonetheless welcome because the conception of that fleeting image more often than not precedes the paintings that flow well from the start and often turn out to be the best I can produce. I guess it is what is known as inspiration! I don't think one should be too analytical about it, the well of inspiration, like hope, springs eternal and that surely is enough to be grateful for.

In my earlier years of painting I worked far more outside on location, always feeling my way through a painting whilst progressing at speed, working spontaneously and instinctively. It led to a great many failures and of course some successes, but it took a few years to learn the value of prior thinking time. Maybe age and experience has had its effect on the realisation that my morning walks and those

The Studio door. Note the 'Beware of Trains' sign

moments spent on the seat by the church porch have become invaluable to the way I work today.

I suppose it could be argued that any planning could well be done in the studio, but somehow for me, and perhaps a little illogically, the distance seems more beneficial to clear thinking and there are, after all, many more distractions within the walls of my studio. It stands in the garden of the eighteenth-century cottage we bought in 1970, just a year after I started to paint full-time. The studio then was a row of semi-derelict stables but the vision of what it might become over the ensuing years has indeed transpired to be all I could have hoped for.

It took some time within the early years of a professional career as an artist to develop the studio into the sort of environment I wanted to create. I had visited the studio of the artist Terence Cuneo, which was filled with artifacts from his worldwide travels. A barn conversion attached to his house in Surrey, it was just full of atmosphere, and a very comfortable place in which to work. His two easels stood either side of the open fireplace and often he would work on the one in the morning, changing

Looking towards the farther room where the easel and watercolour table are.

The 'working' end

after lunch and a snooze on the sofa, to the painting on the other easel for the afternoon.

I am not sure that I could follow his methods of working on two paintings at the same time but I am sure his studio had a great influence on the way my own studio has developed – its three rooms have over the years become filled with reminders of my own travels both here and overseas.

Just by the chair where I sit to write is a lovely old cabin trunk, a present from my wife. Its leather surface has a beautiful patina born of its age and travels. On each side are the original Cunard labels that speak of the times of the great liners in the 1920s and '30s. I love the romance that is held within it. Who owned it I wonder? And where did it travel to? New York? The Greek Islands? Or perhaps on the Orient Express to the wonderful city of Venice?

Just the mention of the name Venice sends a glow of pleasure through my veins. It very quickly became one of my most favourite places to visit and paint after my first trip there in 1993. Consequently the studio holds a great many objects that recall my yearly visits. Amongst them is an old French book entitled *Two Months of Holidays in Italy*, which surprisingly opens up to reveal a miniature set of cupboards and drawers, their contents depicting artifacts from the Grand Tour of travellers of the past. On the cabin trunk are placed a pair of ladies shoes, but again these are no ordinary shoes – they are intricately carved in pine, their style reflecting the same era as the trunk itself, and are the work of the Venetian wood carver, Loris Marazzi.

Have paints, will travel

I will come back to Venice a little later but in the meantime I would not want to give the impression that I have travelled widely – a handful of countries at the most, eight or nine maybe, having preferred to revisit different areas of the countries that Mary and I have enjoyed and in which I have found much to paint. Airports hold no pleasure for me whatsoever and if an alternative to flight can be found then I am the happier for it. Trains and train travel have always been a fascination. The great age of the steam locomotive has been an enthusiasm since boyhood and, as life and my painting career developed, the age of steam became a compelling subject for my brushes, and is so to this day.

Now of course, rail travel to the continent is somewhat easier since the opening of the Channel Tunnel when with one fell swoop a journey can be taken from England to France without getting out of one's seat. The days of the 'Golden Arrow' and the great boat-trains such as 'The Cunarder' are an historic part of railway history, glamourous names from the past when luxury travel was provided in Pullman cars with first-class catering facilities.

The zenith of the boat-train was seen in the 1920s and '30s but some services survived into the 1980s in a reduced form. That glamourous image of the best of the boat-trains has of course been reintroduced to us with the resurrection of perhaps the best known name of all, 'The Orient Express'. It offers a fascinating way to travel to Venice in those chocolate and cream Pullman cars on this side of the Channel, and the sumptuous art-nouveau luxury of the *wagons-lits* coaches in France.

The alternative, if one flies to Venice, is to take the exciting water-taxi ride from the airport across the lagoon at high speed towards the city. I well remember the first time Mary and I arrived along the Grand Canal. It was dusk and the lights from the palaces twinkled and reflected in the water as our craft slowly made its way towards our hotel. The ever-present buzz of activity from the Venetians, the tourists' gondolas, the music and people dining alongside the water, against a backdrop of the most amazing architecture in the world, all combined to make unforgettable images of that evening arrival.

Mary thought it was all so romantic and I could hardly disagree. To see it for the first time in that light at dusk was indeed pure magic.

Our first trip to the continent, however, was to the Greek Island of Ithaca in 1989. Ithaca is a lush green island, pretty and then quite unspoilt by tourism. I recall it came as something of a shock to realise that the majority of colours in my palette were those more suitable to the English landscape. On Ithaca I needed a mauve, some cerulean blue, lemon yellow and a pink, all colours I had not found a use for previously. My palette until then had consisted of the earth colours – the ochres, siennas and browns, with blues such as prussian and ultramarine.

Those extra colours have remained in my colour-box for work either here or abroad and just a few of the paintings from my visits to Ithaca in both 1989 and 1990 are reproduced in contrast to the later work done in Italy and France.

Other countries illustrated in this book include Norway and Belgium. Bruges is a particularly delightful city with much to paint along its canals, although its atmosphere and architecture have a very different feel to that along the canals of Venice. In Bruges the canals are quieter, more serene, and of course more verdant, with trees lining many of the streets alongside the canal system; but I think there are more contrasts than there are similarities with Venice.

'The Orient Express'
Oil Painting 18" x 24"

Heading through a winter landscape the glamour of what is perhaps the most famous train in the world is seen here in its heyday when steam traction was universal.

The Simplon-Orient Express was inaugurated in 1919 and ran from Paris to Constantinople, now Istanbul. It called at Lausanne, Milan, Venice, Trieste, Zagreb, Belgrade, Nish and Sophia, a journey of some fifty-six hours.

The last run of the original Orient Express was made on 19 May 1977, but it was a sad shadow of its former glory, and arrived in Istanbul over five hours late.

In fact one of my intentions in selecting the paintings for this book was to create pictorial contrasts. Contrasts within the continental pictures from the snows of the Alps to the heat of Siena, and contrasts between the overseas paintings and those done within our shores. The English, Welsh and Scottish paintings will display a more earthy palette. The siennas and umbers with warmer greens will reflect the colours under our British skies.

Wales has long since been an inspiration. I remember my visit to North Wales at the age of fourteen – it was indeed an eye-opener seen as it was from the pillion seat of my father's Royal Enfield motor cycle combination. I shall always remember the excitement I felt on seeing the hills of Berwyn and Llangollen, later to be superseded in grandeur by the Mountains of Snowdonia. To a boy from the relatively flat county of Leicestershire it was indeed awe-inspiring. Later, in the 1960s and '70s I saw quite a bit of South Wales and painted much of its coal-mining industry. As the mines closed so the subjects became more compelling. The dereliction and waste as another of our great industries ground to a halt made for paintings full of drama and pathos.

In fact there is so much variety to paint within the United Kingdom that one sometimes feels that there is very little need to venture abroad at all! But there is no doubt that to do so does expand an artist's vision, particularly in the fields of colour and light, and of course it also feels good occasionally to have that continental sun on one's back! But it is memories such as those I have described that are so often triggered by turning the pages of my many sketchbooks. All the sketches are dated, together with a note of where they are, so in fact each book works exactly like a diary – evoking vivid memories of the day, the time, the weather, what happened whilst I was working on the drawing, and of course who I was with. Some of my notes that accompany the paintings will illustrate this point for there is a story to go with most paintings one way or another. I have selected some of these sketches to accompany the paintings although of course they are reduced in scale from the A4 size of my sketch books. The A4 page is a good size to work on – big enough for detail and held easily, even when seated having a coffee in a café in the sunshine!

Apart from a period in my younger years of the 1960s, when I painted abstracts and then pop-art pictures, I have never thought of myself as anything other than a painter of the English School, particularly so where watercolour is concerned, and perhaps the number of watercolours reproduced throughout these pages will reflect that it is certainly my favourite medium and the one I have used more and more over the last few years.

It stems from two things; my love of the British countryside and an enthusiasm for the work of those nineteenth-century masters of watercolour who set such a high standard for the medium. I have learnt much from studying their work as of course I have from those whom I admire of the present day who work along similar lines to myself inspired by nature and by colour and light.

Too often these days traditional painting is dismissed by many within the art world as being of little effect. The argument being that it says nothing new. That may well be so of course but what can be wrong with celebrating what we see with our hearts and eyes within the admittedly simplistic language of traditional art?

I had my three or four year brush with abstraction and what may have been considered to be the more thought provoking forms of self expression but returned naturally, if by degrees, to the more 'conservative' form of expression in traditional painting. It was right for me, and came from the heart as all good painting must do.

My technique or way of painting has developed over some fifty-seven years now and has naturally gone through much experimentation in the process. It is based on sound drawing which is where those sketch books I mentioned earlier come in. In working on a drawing outside much is absorbed about the subject as the eye travels over every inch of it, so that when it comes to using the sketch, no matter how long afterwards, most of the painting will have already been worked out in the mind's eye.

Technique, of course, should develop naturally, it should not be copied or invented for there will be little virtue in that. The influence of other painters will undoubtedly play its part and that is as it should be. My own line of descent, as it were, stems from Cotman, Girtin and Prout, through to Singer Sargent and then Edward Seago, Jack Merriot and Claud Buckle. From my contemporaries, amongst others, I much admire the work of Trevor Chamberlain and David Curtis. All these painters were or are concerned with light, perhaps above all. Each conveys emotion and atmosphere in their work and every one of them shows fine draughtsmanship.

In this book I revel in the glories of Venice and in the sheer colour, light and at times exuberance of the Italian and French subjects seen through an English eye. The contrasts with the paintings done in the British Isles, and those of the low countries, both in light and subject matter, is often quite dramatic and I hope that this collection of paintings with its great diversity of subjects will to some extent reflect the exciting and variable nature of my everyday painting life.

David Weston
The Lazy Acre, Kirby Bellars

The Stove

Watercolour 10"x7"

This subject couldn't be closer to home, in fact it depicts the rusty stove in the old wheelwright's shop at the Lazy Acre. Together with the phone on the wall it caught my eye one day when the light hit it just so, and this was the result.

I applied a lot of restraint in doing it and let some basic ink drawing do much of the work.

ENGLAND

The paintings in this first section can only reflect a few of the many places where I have found the inspiration to paint and have returned to again and again.

The counties of Norfolk and Suffolk are very close to my heart. The little towns of Aldburgh and Southwold reflect an air of the past and are architecturally delightful. The fishing creek of Walberswick close by, with its ramshackle fishing sheds and clutter of boats and tackle has drawn artists back to its water's edge for a century or more.

From Cumbria through Yorkshire, down to Devon and Cornwall, the landscape and character of England changes dramatically, and with it of course the rich and diverse nature of our architectural heritage which I would venture to suggest would be hard to beat in any other European country.

Architecture features largely in the paintings reproduced here. Country houses and churches contrast with the industrial buildings and the industrial scene as a part of the England I know so well and love to paint. So much sets me alight. Canals with their folk art and distinctive architecture, coal mines, steelworks, fishing creeks and beach huts by the seaside. Windmills and watermills, or the bluff stone buildings of Yorkshire to contrast with the lapboard structures of the Kent coast. Norfolk flint and red pantiles. Blacksmiths' forges and old wheelwrights' shops – where they can still be found. And railways of course – the great age of the British Steam locomotive which brought with it, for me at least, the inspiration to portray their splendour and quirkiness on canvas by the bucketful!

Such is the diversity of the English scene that I have separated the paintings into two sections, here and at the end of the book, returning home after the many contrasts within the work I have produced overseas.

When I first ventured out with paints and sketching materials way back in the 1950s at the age of fourteen I had a natural love of nature and the landscape I had been born into. The woods and rolling landscape of Leicestershire, together with its villages, was where I found my initial inspiration, but soon I found that the city also had its attractions where subjects to paint were concerned. On page 23 the painting 'Light on the Old Grand Union', painted in 2005 from a drawing done in the early 1960s, is representative of many subjects that may be found to this day on the inner-city canals of industrial England.

Such aspects of England and English life so often reflect its industrial decline, a recurring theme in much of my work over the years. These paintings are not based on nostalgia. They are simply statements of how things were or are.

There is so much to enjoy and paint within the English countryside that inspiration to work is never far away – crabpots on a quayside or a quiet corner of a sunlit church, the list is endless and always very rewarding.

Breaking Light, Pin Mill
Watercolour 11" x 18.5"

Over the Bridge, Blickling
Watercolour 13" x 5"

In this line and wash painting of the façade of Norfolk's Blickling Hall I wanted to catch the beautiful rose-coloured brick in both sunlight and shadow. In sun it takes on a distinct deep pink whereas in shade the richer more umber-mauve shades are prominent, creating lovely contrasts and also harmonies.

Blickling is one of England's most beautiful houses from the Jacobean period It was built for the Lord Chief Justice, Sir Henry Hobart, between 1616 and 1625. Now cared for by The National Trust, its lake and gardens provide a magnificent setting for this most splendid of Norfolk's country houses.

Watering Cans, Cracoe, Yorks
Oil 8.5" x 7.5"

Boats and Sheds at Southwold
Watercolour 11″ x 15.5″

Fishing Gear at Hope Cove
Watercolour 12.5" x 9.5"

Pithead
Watercolour 11.5" x 15.5"

The dramatic form of this long-disused winding gear at Pleasley in Nottinghamshire made a great impact on me and resulted in this painting. The mine had been in operation since 1871 and had one of the deepest shafts in the Midlands coalfields, descending 1000 yards.

Pleasley has proved to be a great mine to paint and is now in the stages of preservation for the future. This painting, however, is a powerful symbol of the decay and dereliction that set in after the pit's closure in 1983.

Autumn Pulpit

Watercolour 12.5" x 9"

This lovely old pulpit, with its stand of Autumn flowers, caught my eye in the little church of Norfolk's Burnham Overy Town. Not that this is a town - this ancient church is surrounded by no more than a handful of cottages and is dedicated to Saint Clement, the Patron Saint of Sailors.

It is the oldest church within the seven parishes of the Burnhams, whose seafaring histories include the birthplace of Admiral Lord Nelson, at Burnham Thorpe.

From the outside the church has a rather French look to it, with its squat tower and pretty little bell cupola. But inside it is essentially English – an atmospheric interior of white walls, spacious, bare, but still very inviting. I kept this watercolour as simple as possible to get across that feeling of space and light.

Silvery Light in the Forge
Watercolour 11.5" x 8.5"

I just love these industrial interior subjects and this one in an old Lincolnshire blacksmith's shop was a little gem with the lovely silvery light bursting in through the open door.

The clutter of tools on and around the anvil and the vice and other equipment beyond only hint at the years of disuse here since the days of the last war.

I was lucky enough to be invited to sketch and paint in this forge when it was first opened up after all those years. The light bouncing on the floor threw the anvil into a lovely silhouetted shape and highlighted the worn cobbles and slabs of the floor.

Steaming Out of Lincoln
Oil Painting 18" x 24"

Lincoln has always been one of my favourite Midlands' cities to draw and paint. The Cathedral and its environs are very beautiful and unspoilt as was at one time the area surrounding Brayford pool. Unfortunately the grand old warehouses and older properties that once gave this area great charm and complemented the upper parts of the city have fallen prey to the vandalism of city planners and modern ugly architecture. The worst of all is a leisure complex overlooking the water. Someone should be jailed for that!

The railways of the city were, and still are, a worthwhile hunting ground for subjects to paint. In this picture a dirty class B1 locomotive hauls its train of wagons out of the city in an atmospheric evocation of steam towards the end of the era. The Cathedral catches the light in the far distance, exactly pinpointing the location which otherwise might have been anywhere in an industrial part of a city's railway system.

Light on the Old Grand Union
Watercolour 13" x 18"

This subject goes back to my younger years when the old Great Central line crossed the canal in the centre of Leicester. This bridge has long since gone and the distant Slater Street cast iron bridge, which was remarkably handsome, has been replaced with a modern concrete structure with no consideration for aesthetic appeal.

This painting was done in 2005 but shows the scene as I saw it and drew it in the 1960s. It was a day I well remember when that lovely gentle light reflected in the water and filled the scene with light and colour. Beauty in industry. But one never forgets a particular light – once seen it remains in the mind's eye for ever.

Sundown on the Estuary
Watercolour 8.5" x 13"

Sunsets can be tricky things to paint – too garish and it looks awful, too pretty and it becomes a chocolate box. So I choose my subjects sunset-wise carefully. What I liked about this one was the boat disappearing into the dusky light of the river bank – only half seen, and then of course the glow from the lowering sun.

The setting is on the Norfolk coast at Burnham Overy Staithe although it could be practically anywhere in England.

Into the Light, Walberswick
Watercolour 9" x 13"

Old Barn at Heydon
Watercolour 10.5" x 15.5"

Somehow I can never resist the temptation to draw an old Land Rover and this one, half hidden by weeds and diffused light was a subject I could not miss. The light, of course, was the real subject. That bright white glow seen through the ragged remains of corrugated iron and rotting wood in a sagging tumbledown shed attracted me instantly.

To produce the scene as I saw it, I used a fairly dark grey paper with the intention of using white gouache to create the strong light. All the rest of the picture is painted in low tones, allowing for the grey paper to affect the watercolour washes and their tonal values.

The Wreck on the Marsh
Watercolour 10" x 20"

I wonder how long this old stager has lain here, slowly rotting away in a little gully on the marsh at Thornham in Norfolk? When was it abandoned and by whom? Such questions motivate me into drawing and painting subjects like this one in which the deserted nature of the scene and the atmosphere of the marsh and sky make a bleak land-scape, yet one of colour and light.

The focal point of the boat – its paint long faded, its timbers rotting and broken – sits comfortably in the land-scape and is slowly disappearing into it. Each winter gale takes its toll on what is left of a once proud sea-going vessel.

WALES

It was a boiling hot day in the first week of May 1953. With a rather vague hand-drawn map, I climbed laboriously up through pine woods and along rocky ridges overlooking the Vale of Crafnant in search of a guest house somewhere on the hills above me. I was lumbered with an all-to-heavy rucksack with a thick roll of paper sticking out of the top like a chimney, and only a faint hope that I was actually heading in the right direction.

My destination was to be a remote farmhouse somewhere above the Conway Valley known as Penrallt, and this, if I ever found it, was to be the start of a whole week painting in the company of others I had yet to meet. For me, then at the age of 18, it was indeed a great adventure. It was the first time I had ventured out on holiday without my parents! Today that must sound rather silly in an age when young people set off backpacking around the world earning their keep as they go, but back in 1953 such a thing as that would have been almost unheard of.

Painting holidays were not common either in the early '50s. I had heard about this one through my local sketch-club and decided, in spite perhaps of an all-too-sheltered upbringing, to give it a go. Eventually my climb from the valley was rewarded with my first sight of the whitewashed house called Penrallt. After a warm welcome from the organiser Arthur Morris and some fellow guests, I was shown to the accommodation which was in wooden chalets, or perhaps I should say sheds, which were without either heat or light. So the prospect of undressing by candlelight on frosty nights in early

May in the heart of the Welsh hills promised to be a bit chilly!

The house, however, offered a little more comfort with a dining room and lounge downstairs, lit in the evenings by pressure oil lamps and most cheeringly, a log fire. As to the guests, I suppose there would be fifteen or so of us altogether. There were some professional people – a doctor and his wife, a photographer, an ophthalmic surgeon, and so on – down to myself who had escaped from my job as a trainee window dresser. But we all shared a great love of painting and also a love of the Welsh hills which were to be our inspiration to paint.

There was no tutor for the holiday – just an enthusiastic spirit which as the week progressed bound us together to such an extent

Painting holiday, Penrallt, 1953. There were not many young people there!

that that first week was to become repeated year after year with many returning, as I did, each May for another injection of the same tonic.

I learnt much from those weeks in the Welsh hills; my work was pretty raw in the early years and some who came were experienced painters. I remember Keeley Brazier from Barmouth who showed me a great deal, and the Welsh sculptor, Jonah Jones, who for several years came along at the end of each week to give us a criticism on our pictures and this was always very enjoyable and helpful.

The evenings at Penrallt were usually most stimulating. After supper we would arrange our day's work around the room for all to see and discuss. Often we would talk well into the night until we could no longer see across the room for a deep blue haze which consisted of the fumes from the oil lamps, mingling with a copious amount of cigarette smoke - a lethal mix I imagine. Sooner or later a decision would be taken to fling open all the doors and windows to clear it - but it usually had the effect of clearing the artists off to their beds at the same time, candles in hand in pitch blackness to our sheds. It was all rather primitive but exciting and a world away from the hectic city life I knew in the middle of the twentieth century. Motor cars of course were not owned by the majority in the early '50s, but some of the better-off had come in their cars, maybe four or five. So when it was decided that a day out to the high peaks of Snowdonia would be nice, a procession of cars set off along the gated one-track road by Llyn Geirionydd with us all tightly packed in.

As we proceeded a shepherd who happened to be near one of the gates opened it and immediately whipped off his cap to stand with bowed head thinking that such a procession could only be a funeral! A rarity indeed to see so many cars at one time in that area of Wales and what bliss it was too to experience such totally unspoilt countryside where the only vehicle in a whole day would be that of the postman.

Mary and I made the mistake of returning to the lake in more recent times in the hope of rekindling some of our memories for the place. But as we approached, cars were parked everywhere. Jet-skis and power-boats raced the length of the water and the noise was horrific. To find such a lovely spot so blighted by such activity was awful and sent us hurriedly on our way to find the lonely little church of Llanrhychwyn. High above the Conway Valley it is enclosed by old yews and weathered oaks.

Although the church dates mainly from the fifteenth century, one enters its simple white interior through an impressive 800 year-old door which slopes out towards you, and then when pushed over its axis is prone to slam back sharply on to the inner wall. I remember

the first time this happened startled sheep bolted from between the pews, startling me into the bargain. It is an interior with only a railed alter table, a simple pulpit and rough stone walls and I have done several paintings of it over the years. Unchanged for centuries there is true solitude and a real sense of peace within its ancient walls.

On the footplate at the Ffestiniog Railway.

There are so many memories of the Penrallt days. I learnt a lot about painting plein-air in watercolour and as the years progressed so did the size of my paintings, with full Imperial becoming the usual. Walking for miles with that huge folder was not always easy, not to say, at times, hazardous. A great storm blew up one day when some of us were at Llyn Idwal, high in the mountains above the Nant Ffrancon pass. We were all drenched within minutes and fled to the cars, but as I was crossing a slate bridge over a waterfall the wind caught my folder like a sail and over I went. Soaked to the skin, it was a miserable journey back to base.

Such are the joys of painting outside in all weather but somehow it is even more rewarding when one returns with something worthwhile, having fought the elements to produce it. How different those painting holidays seem now to the well-organised ones I see advertised in the magazines of today. Top class hotels with excellent tutors seem to be a requirement for most and it has all become a big industry with hundreds of alternatives offered each year, some in the most exotic locations that would make my adventures in the North wales of the 50s seem like child's play, although I hardly think a candle-lit shed would quite draw in the customers in this day and age!

I have of course returned to Wales many times since those earlier years and made many friends there which have resulted in one-man shows in Cardiff, Portmadoc, Penrhyn Castle and Llanberis, with a large retrospective exhibition at Oriel Ynys Mon on Anglesey in the year 2000.

It remains a part of the world very close to my heart which I trust the paintings will convey. They are only a small selection from the volume of work I have produced in Wales but within them I wanted to show something of both the serene beauty of the landscape and contrary to that the grit and drama of Wales in differing weather conditions.

Old Farm on Anglesey
Watercolour 13" x 21"

The End of the Line at Penrhyn
Watercolour 13.5" x 19.5"

This line of old engines were withdrawn from service and stood outside the shed, their work at the Penrhyn slate quarries having come to an end in the late 1950s. The extensive slate quarries lay just south of Bethesda in Caernarvonshire and these diminutive 0-4-0 saddle-tanks worked on the higher levels of the quarries, some of them having been built as early as the 1880s.

I remember watching these engines at work in the 1950s and wherever one painted in the Bethesda area or at Llanberis where the Dinorwic quarries were in operation, one could hear these engines high on the mountainsides, running along their galleries carved into the quarry face, the highest at Dinorwic being at about 2000ft.

The engines hauled the slate in small wagons to cable-worked inclines linking each level and so the slate was lowered to the base of the mountainside. From there the Dinorwic slate was taken by their company's private rail lines to Port Dinorwic with its scenic route alongside Llyn Padarn, and from the Bethesda quarries to Port Penrhyn – the departure points for Welsh slate to be exported throughout the world.

I tried to keep this watercolour as loose as possible whilst not losing too much detail on the nearer engines, the shed in the background being left more drawn than painted together with the third locomotive in the line. Some very loose wash-work was all that was required to suggest the abandoned nature of the scene.

The Foot of the Pass, Llanberis
Watercolour 8" x 12"

The Barclay at Merthyr Vale
Watercolour 12" x 19"

There is high drama in this full strength watercolour set in the Welsh coalfields at Merthyr Vale. The battered old engine built by Andrew Barclay & Co looks as though it was probably on its last legs but somehow has been kept going by the expertise of the little band of engineers at the colliery.

The headstocks always make a dramatic statement at any pit and here the pair combine with the buildings below to make an intriguing background to the engine – just catching the light on its cab and side tanks with some lovely colour and that small touch of red on the buffer beam which is so important. Too much would have been disastrous.

My visits to South Wales, particularly in the 1960s, gave me access to many colliery sites and in the years since, dozens of paintings have resulted from those trips. The two reproduced here are more recent paintings produced from the sketches done at that time.

Dark and Light at Black Rock Sands
Oil Painting 10" x 14"

Silent Interior, Llanrhychwyn church
Watercolour 10" x 13"

The Wilds of the Hirnant Pass
Watercolour 12.5" x 20.5"

In this moody watercolour of a dramatic piece of the Welsh landscape I wanted to create not only the atmosphere of the day and place but also the vastness of this wild and exciting valley with its meandering stretch of single track road diminishing into the far distance.

The Hirnant pass runs from the Northern end of Lake Vyrnwy through almost to Bala and is one of the most exciting bits of pure landscape I have come across. There is not a house or farm to be seen in the painting and the drops down from the road are at times a little concerning, but on a day of variable cloud when the light chases through the valley it is a truly magnificent landscape.

Tin Barn
Watercolour 9" x 13"

For me painting North Wales is about two very different things. One is the sheer beauty of the landscape on a fine day, and the other is about the harshness of that same landscape in poor or bitter weather conditions. Then it is bleak, wet and often desolate.

Farming in such conditions on the exposed highlands must be a hard way of life, and I have tried to express a little of that in this painting. The mist is enclosing the landscape with everything soaked through, and that old barn with its unwelcoming, draughty corrugated iron and broken slate wall makes a dramatic statement in an otherwise empty scene, save for the farmer who has to put up with it and get on with earning his living.

Wales on such days is definitely bleak!

The Road Above Dinorwic
Watercolour 9" x 13"

Returning Home
Watercolour 7.5" x 11"

Coal, Smoke and Steampower
Watercolour 13" x 19"

By the Shores of Llyn Llydaw
Watercolour 13" x 19"

For most people the ascent of Snowdon by the miners' track offers a walk as far as Llyn Llydaw before the climb becomes a little more severe on its way up to Llyn Glaslyn and beyond.

The lake is crossed by a causeway and its dark green waters reflect copper deposits from the mining activities of the past. On a dull day it can be a gloomy spot - the great height of Lliwedd towers over the scene. But on a day of broken cloud, as in this painting, patches of light illuminate alternate areas and the peaks are lost and found as the clouds break and soften their harsh and dramatic lines.

The ruins of the old copper mine make a great focal point for this composition in which I have used an ink line on both the buildings and foreground. It helps to push the very strong background of the mountain-sides further away and creates a contrast between the hard drawing near-to and the softer lines of the distant rocks drawn with a brush.

I have sketched and painted here in some atrocious weather at times and produced several pictures of this subject over the years. It is one of those that draws me back, always with the hope of getting it bang on one day.

Track to the Devil's Kitchen
Watercolour 9" x 13"

It is an easy climb from Llyn Ogwen in the Nant Ffrancon pass to Llyn Idwal over a well trodden track to this point approaching the shoulder where one gets that first sight of the lake in a bowl of rock, its cliff-faces dropping almost sheer into the water.

I liked this view, not only for the wild nature of the track and the frontal lighting, but it holds a hint of promise. What shall we find when we breast the summit of the path ahead? Is the lake deserted or are there swarms of walkers and climbers already there?

The Devil's Kitchen refers to that cleft in the rock to the right of centre which provides the most dramatic cliff face around Llyn Idwal and a well-used route for climbers. The light was an important factor too in painting this subject. That soft light of the palest of greens on the tops of the far mountain sides was so important to get about right – it gave form and mystery to the distant panorama of those rock-faces that descend to the lake.

Stormclouds over Snowdon
Watercolour 10.5" x 19"

I just love to be in the high mountains on a day like this one when the peaks play hide-and-seek in the clouds. There is such movement and mystery within the landscape and this view is a belter.

It is from the twin lakes of Llynnau Mymbyr and is a spectacular landscape by any standards. The dramatic darks in the middle distance of this painting push the far distance well back and thrust the foreground to the front.

The walkers add interest to the left, stop a sloping line from slipping out the the composition, and give scale to the vastness of the scene.

Fishing at Llyn Craftnant
Watercolour 8" x 13"

Cottage Interior, Bala
Watercolour 9" x 13"

FRANCE

What a wonderfully inspiring country France is for any artist – often it is the quality of the light that makes a French subject so compelling. I cannot of course claim to know the country throughout its length and breadth, but the various regions I know have all offered some very different aspects of this great part of the world. From the Haute Savoir region of the Alps to the Dordogne, or Cassis and Provence in the South to Normandy and Brittany further North, there are so many great contrasts of both scenery and architecture.

I have made many visits to the Haute Savoir area at differing times of the year, often staying in the popular ski resort of Morzine. In winter it is magical when deep snow covers both the mountains and villages, and it is an interesting experience to portray such snow scenes on paper or canvas. I have included one or two here from those visits including some done in the high Alps and on Mont Blanc itself. Sketching at such high altitudes can have its hazards – a friend of mine set his stool down in deep snow only to disappear when he sat on it into a six-foot drift! Nonetheless, painting outside is very exhilarating and unlike the winter snows of Great Britain it is lovely to be able to sit out at times in shirt-sleeves under a warm sun whilst painting in the snow.

Away from the sun, on days when the weather has clamped down in Morzine, I have often been fortunate enough to enjoy painting in a lovely old house called Mas de la Coutettaz (page 65). There are many excellent interior subjects within its walls and as this wonderfully rambling old house is,so I am told, the oldest in Morzine, it has

character in abundance to prove it. Built originally for the owner of a local slate mine its floors display a wonderful variety of their best slate in huge slabs of irregular shapes and sizes. The house is now owned by an Englishman, Dorian Ricardo, whose hospitality I have often been grateful for on those days when the weather in Morzine has been too wet to work outside.

From Morzine Mary and I have many times taken the trip down to Annecy with its beautiful lake and fascinating town through which threads a canal to reflect its typically French architecture. I have included three or four paintings of this lovely old town, although the ones where the canal is featured seem to have escaped reproduction!

Cassis in the South is another lovely town with its many plane trees that cast dappled light throughout its centre and harbourside. My painting of the old bakery (page 58) in a side street just off the harbour brings back memories of the delicious smells whilst I was working on the drawing for it. But apart from that it was the textures on those old walls and the leaning shutters and faded lettering that made me want to paint this fascinating bit of old Cassis.

I have enjoyed all the various regions of France I have painted in, from Provence to the Perignon region of the Dordogne, and to the farmlands and farmsteads of villages close to Geneva.

One thing is always paramount to the success of these paintings and that is that lovely French light. The impressionists revelled in it and painted it so successfully. One can only do one's best, humbly aware of the magnitude of their achievements.

Café in Cassis
Watercolour 11″ x 8.5″

Passage des Nemours, Annency
Watercolour 12.5" x 10.5"

Woodsmoke
Watercolour 12" x 17.5"

Just up from Morzine is the Valley Des Ardroisiere where I found this lovely subject so typical of the architecture of the Haute Savoir area. There was a combination of things to attract me – the cart in front of the house and the rich shadows on the old woodshed were enhanced by the setting of the sheer cliffs in the valley and then the woodsmoke, blowing about to occasionally obscure part of the scene. Oh, and the smell from that pine being burnt! I spent some time here drawing before carrying on up the valley to our destination for lunch.

Winter in Montrionde
Watercolour 13.5" x 19"

Snow at Les Linderets
Watercolour 12" x 18"

There were some lovely contrasts of hot and cold colours in this Alpine scene in the village of Les Linderets, known locally for the dozens of goats that roam freely around its streets.

The warmth of colour in the huts with their cracked and dried-up timbers was the perfect foil to the cool colour of the trees laden with snow The group of walkers rivet the eye and make a great focal point in the space between the buildings - their placing was critical but grouped with the right hand barn they balance the composition of the whole scene very well.

Lunchtime in Annecy
Oil Painting 16" x 12"

Annecy is a place of brilliant sunshine and deep shadows. Its warm stone and cream or white painted façades bounce off the light to create great contrasts of warm and cool colours.

In this scene the lunchtime tables themselves reflect the light and make a glittering display in a composition where the focus is on the people rather than the architecture, despite the striking light effects through the archway.

The area of deep shade in the foreground of this painting has been kept relatively empty save for a chair or two in a half light, leaving lots for the imagination of the viewer. I love Annecy, and this scene typifies much of what I enjoy so much about it.

The House at Le Biot
Watercolour 9" x 13"

Piano Piece
Watercolour 12" x 9"

A morning sun lit this interior in the dining room of an old wooden house we were staying in at Morzine. I was struck by the way the light hit the piano, and the restricted colour scheme of the whole scene, the softness of the drapes contrasting perfectly with the hard lines of the wood walls and furniture.

The painting reminds me of an incident very early on in my professional career when at the time I had a small shop-come-studio in Leicester. I had painted a very large railway picture which was some three feet in height by about four or five feet long. It hung on the back wall opposite the window and being of some considerable size would have had, for its day, a hefty price tag on it.

Amongst those who admired it was an elderly chap from the foundry down the road. He came in overalls and the dirtiest flat cap I had ever seen. But his fascination with the painting was absolute. Each time he came in he profusely apologised for the intrusion, gazed at the painting for anything up to a full ten minutes and left asking if I minded if he came in again?

He did, several times, until one day he asked me how much such a painting would cost? My answer led him to grab the table for support saying that in no way could he afford such an amount, but did I mind if he returned to just look at it again? Well of course I didn't, after all that is why any painting is done – to give pleasure or to make an impression on others.

It might have been or week or so later when the door was pushed open just as I was about to lock up for the night, and there he was again apologising for bothering me. Still in his overalls and cap he carried a small bag in which was his flask and sandwich tin, which as usual he placed on the table. Then after some minutes of looking at the reason for his visits he took out the sandwich tin from the bag. I really thought he was going to settle down for the night, but no! Inside the tin were hundreds of crumpled-up notes. "Here", he said, "I'm going to have to have it. Count them out shall you, I think its about right".

To say that I was astonished is no exaggeration and had agreed to actually deliver it before I realised that it was a bit big to go on my bike! Later that week my friend the butcher's boy, who was just around the corner, brought his boss's van round and with a bit of juggling we got the picture in.

We arrived at a terraced house where we were summoned from behind some dusty nets to take the painting down the entry to the back door. From there we were ushered in through to the front parlour which was in total disarray with so much furniture and what I can only call junk that it was a job to put the picture down anywhere. "Do you mind hanging it for me?" my customer asked. "I'll have it up there behind the piano". One glance at the aforementioned piece of furniture nearly stumped us. It was absolutely piled high with old newspapers, Guinness bottles, books, lamps, a first aid box (that looked as if it might come in handy!), and years and years of dust.

Somehow it had to be shifted out into an already overcrowded space but with much coughing and sneezing we managed it. The painting was hung from a picture rail and was obviously too low on the wall, but was as high as we could get it. I asked where the piano was going? "Oh just shove it back, it won't go anywhere else". Having carried out the instruction we stood back to see two-thirds of the painting completely hidden behind the piano! Just the sky and a bit of smoke remained visible. I asked if he wanted us to help clear the top off. "Oh Lord, no master, it will only go back on if you do" .

To view what was left of my painting through a conglomeration of rubbish and Guinness bottles totally defeated me but my client was happy and when I mentioned that not too much of the painting could be seen he said with a great sigh of satisfaction, "Ah, but I know it's there".

I have sold a great many paintings since that experience from my early days as a professional artist, but never another to hang behind a piano... Well, not that I know of!

Down the Stair
Watercolour 12" x 8"

This interior is set in a chateau in the Dordogne. We had been out for a long walk and as I mounted the stairs to our room I threw my hat on to the banister rail. On coming down some time later I was struck by the way it just made this subject.

The light flooded in through the open door, just catching the sewing machine, and reflected brilliantly on the polished floor and the newel post of the staircase. The hat, perhaps foreign to the rest of the scene, became a great focal point and adds to the suggestion here of that hot afternoon sun.

Farmyard at Thoiry
Watercolour 19.5" x 13.5"

Cart Sheds at Le Biot
Watercolour 10.5" x 16"

I found these wonderful old sheds in the little mountain village of Le Biot in the Haute Savior region of France. The whole scene had almost a 'wild west' look to it but I liked the shapes of the wooden buildings and those lovely lamps that stood out against the pale hillside.

In the foreground shed is an old horse-drawn timber carriage, used by woodsmen for transporting felled trees. It was loaded with huge balks of timber and I think had not been moved for some years.

The Bakery at Cassis
Watercolour 9.5" x 8.5"

Cote Nemours, Annency
Watercolour 13.5" x 8.5"

Morning in the Dordogne
Watercolour 13" x 19"

We had taken a walk of some miles along little used roads through farms and fields in heavenly countryside, and stopped to befriend this little pony who took quite a liking to Mary and Janet.

This view is typical of the landscape in the Perignon region of the Dordogne, rather like the Cotswolds in many ways, but totally unspoilt and of course more vast.

I was struck by the glowing colour of the harvest fields when we were there – quite stunning compared to the colour usually seen in Britain. It is only hinted at in this painting but I liked the casual nature of the farm buildings in the landscape and the setting of the whole scene.

Le Citroën
Watercolour 9" x 13"

What a find! This lovey old Citroën, a car that is so much a part of France's social and automobile history and an icon of its age. But as if the car itself was not enough, just look at that shed. How it ever survived the slightest breath of wind I cannot imagine. But it made great pictorial material and I just loved painting this scene - but then I do have a certain penchant for old cars. That aside, the textures and the colours in those random planks of wood were so varied, some long since painted and faded, others just natural.

The wonky staircase and the yellow flowers also added more than somewhat to the interest of this unusual subject.

Escalier du Chateau, Annency
Watercolour 15" x 13.5"

On the Front at Yvoire
Watercolour 14" x 21"

After Supper at the Chateau
Oil Painting 16" x 12"

I saw this scene, full of glittering and reflected lights in the Chateau we were staying in at Villars in the Dordogne. My three friends, finishing off their cheese and biscuits, were chatting happily, unaware of the subject they were creating for me. The strong evening light reflected in the floor-boards and just caught the foreground table with its books and wine glass. The deep shadow at the front emphasises the light beyond, creating some lovely silhouettes and a great sparkle of light on the dining table. I have to say, this is one I was pleased with.

Mas de la Coutettaz, Morzine
Oil Painting 16" x 12"

On the Ascent of Mont Blanc
Watercolour 13.5" x 21"

BRUGES, BELGIUM

I have often heard Bruges referred to as "the Venice of the North", due to the canal systems that run throughout the town. But there I think any other possible similarity must end. The architecture is of course very different, although some is just as spectacular and splendid. But the whole atmosphere and feeling of Bruges is one of a more relaxed and peaceful nature than that felt in much of Venice.

The Flemish style of architecture dating from the fifteenth to the eighteenth century dominates the town but there are also many wonderful buildings that represent the past from as far back as the Middle Ages.

It is a lovely experience to sit at one of the many cafés in the spacious market square to simply observe the comings and goings of what is the busiest part of town. And if architecture is your bag then the extraordinary mix of styles around the square will be a delight to the eye. It is overlooked by the great bell tower which houses a carrillion of some forty-seven bells that play well known tunes at regular intervals.

But I must not let my enthusiasm for architecture spill over, for Bruges is about much more. Here in the square the carriage rides gather to await their custom, adding considerably to the atmosphere and colourful interest of the market place. As one would take a gondola ride in Venice, so in Bruges it is the horse and carriage that takes the visitor on a conducted tour through the cobbled streets of the town's centre which echo to the clip-clop of hooves, making a constant and pleasing sound. It is an excellent way to familiarise oneself with the layout of the town and a glimpse of the places one might go back to again on foot.

The paintings I have produced of Bruges on the whole depict those quieter areas of town, the streets alongside the canals are only minutes walk away from the busy town centre, but they are a world away in terms of atmosphere.

I love these areas in the early morning. There is a wonderful golden light that is magnificent when seen on the canals that run roughly from east to west, and when it is accompanied by a slight mist the effects are sheer magic.

Bruges is a place of many surprises and the fact that it is so easy to get around on foot makes it all the more relaxing and interesting. A lovely tree-lined walk encircles the town, passing the old city gates and three or four windmills. Trees are a big feature in this town, softening the hard lines of the Flemish architecture and casting dappled light on their varied surfaces. The stepped gables of painted façades look down on cobbled streets that dip and bend, sometimes at alarming angles. Over the canals are brick and stone bridges of simple but handsome proportions, spanning the water whose reflections are only broken by the occasional tourist boat.

Here one can paint or draw at any time of day in comfort throughout the year, although of all the seasons in Bruges I like autumn the best when the trees turn to oranges and golds, dropping their leaves on the ground, adding even more colour to an already vibrant townscape.

Morning on Groen Rei
Watercolour 11.5" x 11.5"

Early Morning Light, Gouden Handrei
Watercolour 11" x 9.5"

Sunlight by Maestraat Bridge, Bruges
Watercolour 13" x 18.5"

A very strong morning sun brilliantly lit the fascias of the houses along Groen Rei and made vivid reflections in the waters of the canal. It caused some dramatic contrasts of light and shade, throwing the bridge and foreground trees and walls into near silhouettes. It is a lovely time to be there, well before breakfast, when few are about and no-one takes any notice of an artist with paints or a sketchbook.

The picture hangs in the home of our friends June and Derek Wright who were with us on this particular trip to Bruges so I see it occasionally. It brings back many memories of that brilliant light that the early morning sun creates in Bruges.

September Fog, Bruges
Watercolour 13" x 18"

An early morning fog on one of the wider stretches of canal in Bruges softened the lines of this old lift-bridge and gave rise to this watercolour done on a damp paper.

I chose a light grey two-rivers paper for this where I could build up tone gently by using careful secondary washes. The colours are basically ultramarine blue mixed with light red to form the greys warmed up a little here and there with a mauve and naples yellow.

Using a restricted palette is good discipline and with a subject like this one where everything is greyed by the atmosphere it is essential. The whole scene required a delicate balance of both warm and cool colours and here of course the autumnal leaves on the trees and ground linked the warmer shades to the roofs and houses on the opposite side of the composition.

Bruges, like Venice in mist or fog, can be quite beautiful - especially in the autumn.

Late Afternoon Light, Bruges
Watercolour 8.5" x 13"

This is the great belfry or Halles Tower that dominates the market square. Seen from this shopping street it made a dramatic statement with the late afternoon sun just catching the buildings at the far end of the street.

The reflections and shadows on the wet road from the silhouetted figures added to the excitement of the scene. It was a painting where a very careful control of colour was paramount to its success, involving a delicate balance between warm, cool and cold shades – a slightly chilly late afternoon in September 2003.

Off to School, Bruges
Watercolour 8.5" x 11.5"

I loved the mix of architectural styles in this street, so typically Bruges. This watercolour was done from a pre-breakfast drawing. There was no one about, and I liked the empty feel of the street, but knew that for the painting a figure would be needed to add life and scale. A mother and child emerged from a nearby door and as I watched them go down the street the pair were just perfectly placed at the corner, and also incidentally gave me my title for the painting.

ITALY

It would be hard to choose between France and Italy as to which was my favourite for painting. They have much in common and yet are completely different. The Italian sun has a sharpness to it that gives a different light to that in France, and yet colour and textures, those bleached out and faded shades on crumbling walls, are often so alike.

Italy is a country of enormous appeal to me as a painter; the lakes of course are all considerably rewarding with subjects in abundance everywhere. Lake Garda is perhaps my favourite and Mary and I usually make a point of staying at the top and more mountainous end of the lake at Riva Del Garda. From there so much is accessible by boat along the lake or away into the hills towards Arco by bus. One of the most beautiful little towns on Lake Garda is Lazise, not so often visited by tourists but truly an absolute gem for an artist. One enters through a gateway in the town walls into a narrow street leading to the central piazza and harbour. It has a typical Italian feel with subjects to paint everywhere. The marble floored Piazza leads down to the lakeside, and although it is one of the smallest places alongside Lake Garda, it is without doubt my favourite.

The lakes of Como and Maggiore are equally beautiful with much to paint, but another of my own favourites is the smaller lake of Orta, with its ancient town square alongside the lake and the dream-like island of San Guillio in its centre. I have included a couple of paintings done in this most delightful of places in this section (pages 80 and 83) which show a little of the architecture, light and atmosphere of the town.

But of course there is much more to Italy than the lakes, their beauty notwithstanding. Each region has its own characteristics –

Tuscany is an area which has provided inspiration for many paintings, but for something totally different the City of Siena is an artists' absolute dream. The great cathedral in black and white marble dominates its area of the centre, and contrasts completely with the red pantiled, stone-built architecture of the rest of Siena. The houses and buildings here are not colourwashed but are for the best part kept in the burnt sienna/raw sienna stone that is natural to the region.

I love the Palazzo Pubblico, the most central Piazza which dips and swoops its way across to the magnificent town hall. From here deep-shaded streets tilt away precariously, their roads and walkways dipping at alarming angles between houses and apartments where almost every occupant seems to own a scooter!

For sheer contrasts between Italian cities there could be none greater than that between Siena and Venice. Venice is a one-off, a city built entirely on water whose history stretches back to the Roman Empire, and a city with a rich cultural and unique architectural heritage.

For a painter, Venice is totally unique with a light that bounces off the water of its canals and on to its crumbling walls. It is a place of faded glories, of ancient palaces that speak of the city's turbulent past, and with a history of art and artists unrivalled anywhere else in the world. The greatest painters from all over the globe came here to pay homage and do so to this day. It is little wonder that the desire in artists to express their inspiration for Venice continues ad-infinitum. With over a dozen visits there myself I felt a separate section of my Venetian paintings was appropriate to follow on from these next pages depicting a few of the glories of Italy.

WESTON.

Afternoon in Arco
Watercolour 11.5" x 15.5"

Via San Anna
Arco 9-6-98

Looking Down on Arco
Watercolour 14.5" x 11"

Arco is a wonderful little town a few miles from Lake Garda and a 'must' for artists. It is overlooked by the remains of a fortress, high above the town, and the steady climb up to it affords some fine views over the landscape and fascinating glimpses over the roofs of the town. In this painting it was the light bouncing on the roofs and on the ground in the square that made me want to paint it. The church of course makes a fine focal point in the composition as the eye is led towards it from several directions.

It is quite a busy painting in contrast to the other one of Arco showing the dramatic cliff and fortress.

Street Scene in Siena
Watercolour 13.5" x 9.5"

In the Villa Capezzara, Carmignano
Watercolour 9" x 13"

Notices in Pisa
Watercolour 12.5" x 18"

Whilst everyone was just around the corner photographing the Leaning Tower I had wandered off in search of something a little less predictable and found this subject.

It is so typically Italian and full of textures - old brick, stone, plaster and aged wood, not to mention the torn and tatty notices, which are in complete contrast to the modern scooter.

Somehow the three main points of interest combined to make a statement about a typical Italian street corner that made the subject well worth doing.

The Town Hall, Orta
Watercolour 9" x 14"

The little square in Orta is where the old town hall with its little white bell tower and faded frescos stands, just begging to be painted or drawn.

Just to the left of the trees in this painting is the lake of Orta which adds to the beautiful feel of this little piazza so fantastically placed on its shore line. I wanted to catch something of the antiquity of the buildings and also the colour of Orta in this painting.

Market in Pistoia
Watercolour 17" x 12.5"

A great build-up of architecture forms the backdrop to this market scene in the Tuscan town of Pistoia. It was irresistible as a subject – I loved the stalls cluttered with fruit boxes and the untidy way the well, with its ancient columns, was totally surrounded with market produce and barrows.

I used a loose brown ink line to define the composition – it is such a busy scene – but one in which I feel I may have caught the essence of an Italian street market with its contrasts of colours, textures and the sun and deep shadow of the day.

In the Piazza, Siena
Watercolour 10" x 16"

The Palazzo Pubblico, seat of government of the Republic of Siena which is now the town hall, forms the central group of buildings in this painting.

I love the way the piazza dips up and down, unlike most Italian open spaces, and the colour of the buildings, unpainted in celebration of the stone – truly the colours of raw sienna and burnt sienna and the umbers.

Siena is a wonderful town. Its cobbled streets plunge down between tall buildings contrasting bright sunlight with an intensity of deep shadow, and then the great Gothic cathedral presents a most striking contrast to the stone of Siena with its black and white marble façade and striped tower.

There is so much to excite the visitor here but sadly I have had too little time so far to see and draw all there is in this intriguing place.

Early Sunlight, Orta
Watercolour 8.5" x 11.5"

A Saturday morning fleamarket surrounded the town hall and cast long deep shadows, cool in the warmth of an early sun. The people, the stalls and the contrasts of light and colour made this a subject that speaks of Italy and was immensely enjoyable to put together.

A Man and His Harley
Watercolour 11" x 19"

A pink Harley Davidson and its laid-back rider taking in the sun at Lazise on Lake Garda. It may be an unusual subject but I enjoyed it enormously – another of my somewhat offbeat subjects.

Of course, it was not just the machine and the storyline in the picture that made me want to do it, important though that is. It is the way the frontal light bounced off the lake to hit the group causing those intriguing shadows that made the whole thing paintable and exciting.

Italian Alleyway
Watercolour 14" x 13"

We were in Limone on the shores of Lake Garda in search of subjects to paint. My friend, who had not long been painting at that time, came out of the alleyway saying that there was nothing there worth a look! 'Seeing' subjects comes with experience and this was a case in point. The contrasts between the glossy blue scooter and its setting was interest enough perhaps, but the archway and its cobbled and textured floor that framed it made it a first class subject from my point of view.

I just loved the patterns the broken floor had evolved into over decades, and the differing shapes and sizes of stone, with a great feeling of antiquity about the whole setting.

Salita Camillo Cavour
Watercolour 16" x 8"

What a great name for this street of steps in Bellagio by Lake Como. I liked the way the steps disappeared, dropping into the cool depth of the shadows by the archway and the misty light coming through.

I debated about having a figure here, but decided against it because I liked the empty feel of the street in the early morning light.

VENICE

There is no city on earth that has drawn more artists to its heart than the great city of Venice. For centuries so little has changed. Just recently I stood facing the Campo dei Frari where John Singer Sargent painted in 1880. His view then, and the one I looked upon, were virtually unaltered. Even the corner shop in his painting is still there, and looks no different today.

This remarkable preservation of Venice's past, both architecturally and historically, is just one of the many aspects of the place that I find so fascinating and rewarding to paint. It may be a little more ravaged by time and flood in the twenty-first century, but no other city could so abundantly display its past at every turn as is the case in Venice.

Canaletto, born in Venice in 1697, was by the 1720s, and for the next thirty years, involved in recording the city for visiting aristocrats on their Grand Tour. So many of his canvases show scenes still familiar to our eyes today.

By the beginning of the nineteenth century British artists were finding their way to the city. In the mid 1820s Richard Parkes Bonington and Samuel Prout were working there, producing paintings that were accurate portrayals of the city's great architecture. But both artists imbued their paintings

Sketching in Venice.

with the magical light for which Venice is revered today. So many such scenes, painted all those years ago, can still be viewed from exactly the same spot those artists chose, and remain almost totally unchanged. The costumes of the figures have altered, the commercial traffic on the canals, the shops and restaurants that now abound, but the basic views are just the same some two-hundred-and-fifty years after Canaletto.

The paintings of Venice I have chosen to include in this book are just a few of the hundreds I have done over the last twelve years or so. Sometimes I have tended to look for the more unusual – fruit boxes outside a shop, a jazz band playing at a café, or torn posters on a wall that hint at the city's cultural life with its great musical and theatrical traditions. Such pictures show something of the present day in Venice but of course I have never been able equally to resist having a go at the 'grand views' such as those along the Grand Canal or in the Piazza di San Marco.

I cannot hope to say anything new about Venice – so much has been painted before, and by so many great artists – but I hope my pictures will show a good diversity of the subjects I have found in this amazing place and in all its many and varied moods.

From the
Fondamenta Van Axel, Venice

Watercolour 17" x 10.5"

This busy scene is set on the Rio Panada. I liked the bustle of the people and the boats and the many and varied textures on the walls of the old palaces in the picture. The slight misting of the buildings beyond the bridge gave the scene that air of mystery that is so often to be found on the Venetian narrow canals.

The Fondamenta Van Axel is but a couple of minutes' walk from the hotel we have sometimes used in the Campo Santa Marina. It is a busy little square where people pass through rather than to linger for long. In the morning one is awakened by the sound of shopkeepers arriving, usually at about 6am! Steel shutters are noisily shot up into their housings and sign boards are dragged out. The Venetians greet each other with their customary shouts. The Italians do not know how to talk at a normal level of conversation. Their voices echo around the square to the accompaniment of a church bell, and then another bell, and somewhere a little distant another bell until the whole city joins in, all its glorious churches welcoming the day.

Unable to sleep any longer, breakfast calls and Venice is once again in full swing. We open our shutters to let in the morning sun and look down on the throngs of Venetians going about their business. Smart businessmen immaculately dressed, stop for a brief conversation. Beautiful young girls in the height of fashion pause at the café opposite for a coffee and croissant. Porters trundle through with huge barrow-loads of fruit and vegetables. Two men carry a sofa to somewhere, and a beggar takes up his pitch by a shaded corner.

It is 7.15am. Yes, Venice is in full swing.

The Quiet of a Venetian Canal
Watercolour 17" x 12"

Passing Storm, San Giovanni e Paolo, Venice
Watercolour 10" x 17"

The magnificent church of San Giovanni e Paolo is an outstanding example of Venice's Gothic religious architecture. The foundation stones were laid in 1246 and the church was finished and consecrated in 1430.

This view of it is from the great bell tower or campanile in the Piazza di San Marco and shows the marble façade of the Scuola Grande of St Mark alongside the church.

We stood and watched the storm as it circled Venice and as it went out and across the lagoon, with the sun still full out over the city. It gave an increased dramatic light which enhanced the architecture of this lovely building and made an exciting composition to do battle with.

Rondo Veneziano, Venice
Watercolour 15" x 12"

I found this pillar whilst walking back to my hotel one night and was bowled over by its colour, its variety of abstract shapes, and of course, its message. I just had to paint it. The deep tones of the thoroughfare leading mysteriously into darkness emphasised the light that hit the pillar and the well-trodden flagstones of the alleyway.

The striking blue poster advertising a concert depicted a group of Venetians at Carnival time – so much part of the city's social and historical background.

Evening Light, Piazza di San Marco
Watercolour 13" x 20"

Venetian Backwater
Watercolour 8" x 13"

Fruit Shop on the Fordamenta san Anna

Watercolour 17" x 13"

Interior, San Giovanni e Paolo
Watercolour 19" x 13"

Light and Shadow on the Grand Canal
Watercolour 12" x 20"

Morning Light, Rio di Tedeschi
Watercolour 20″ x 11″

From Calle Del Forner
Venice
23-9-96

Venetian Façade, Venice
Watercolour 14" x 19"

The faded glory of a one-time grand house made a lovely subject of textures and warm colour. The whole group of windows, door and balcony is offset to the right of the painting – the white washing then not only suggests life but gives, through its importance, an overall balance to the composition.

The Eerie Silence of a Venetian Canal

Watercolour 12" x 9"

Venice at night is always intriguing. In the vast public spaces it can be spectacular, theatrical and dramatic; in the quieter canals, mysterious and atmospheric.

In this watercolour I was keen to capture the stillness of this backwater with its accents of electric lights and dark window shapes reflecting in the inky depth of the canal.

A gondola steals around the corner to temporarily break the stillness. The gondolier's voice echoes off the high walls for only a moment but then the scene returns to that eerie silence that I know so well of the Venetian night.

Nocturnes like this are extremely difficult to get right in watercolour. It has to be done on a damp paper and worked very fast with watercolour at its full strength. Anything can go wrong at any time, especially if one touches a patch of half-dry paper. But here I was lucky and it turned out much as I had envisaged and wanted it to.

1256 Calle Del Campaniel, Venice
Watercolour 19.5" X 12"

On a hot day in the May of 2002 I sat with a trio of friends to sketch this fascinating corner and inevitably, whenever a group of artists set their easels up or open their sketchbooks, it is not long before onlookers gather to offer their opinions. The Venetians largely ignore artists – too common a sight I suppose – but occasionally an Italian voice may be heard to express some admiration with 'che bello, che bello'.

One nods an appreciative glance and a smile in return. Such was the case here when our work caused a slight diversion for inhabitants of the surrounding apartments. Except this time there was an Australian voice that added to the growing throng. It belonged to the lady who lived in the house whose shuttered window I was drawing. Her appreciation was such that within a short while she returned with biscuits and ice-cold drinks for the four of us. Such kindnesses are not uncommon in general, but I have to say are rather less so in Venice.

In this painting of her house I loved the shutters faded blue which contrasted with the warm shades of the rest of the picture. The corner made more vital by the frontal light thrusting down the alleyway with its washing and figures.

So often I love to just savour the sounds of Venice as I sit to draw or paint: the echoing voices of gondoliers as they pass or shout "Hoya, Hoya", on a blind corner; always the bells near and far reverberate across the city; and often near at hand, perhaps on a balcony, a canary trills its joyful song from a gilded cage.

Waiting in the Shade
Watercolour 11" x 8"

I saw this nun sitting on a barrow whilst patiently waiting for a porter to appear. It was in one of my most favourite quiet areas of Venice in the Cannaregio region quite close to the port. The church in the background is the Chiesa S. Nicolo and I liked the contrast of cool and warm colours in the composition and the contrast also between strong sunlight and deep shadow.

As I observed this scene there was a wonderful sense of tranquillity about it that appealed enormously and I have tried to get it into this painting.

WESTON.

The Rialto Market, Venice
Watercolour 13" x 19"

Usually this thoroughfare is so full of people that it is impossible to get a clear view of the stalls. However, an early morning visit is the best option to see the scene as I have painted it here.

The stalls are the real focal point of this composition and I allowed some drawing to escape without much colour on the left of the picture so as to lead the eye in gently to the more contrasting sections.

The market is overlooked by the fascinating church of San Giacometto di Rialto, the oldest in Venice, and makes an imposing backdrop.

Morning Glow, Venice
Watercolour 12" x 8.5"

This was the first painting I ever did of Venice, and it remains a part of our own collection of paintings in the house. It represents the rewards of an early morning walk towards the Campo San Giovanni e Paolo. The golden glow on the buildings along the canal there was such that I have never chanced upon since in that same spot.

The very strong impression it made on me resulted in this very simple watercolour, restricted in the main to browns and golds. I painted very little detail in the buildings because to do so would very likely have diminished the sense of light and atmosphere that was paramount to the image I wanted to convey – one of light; that lovely fresh golden light that bounces off the water to reflect on the surrounding walls on an early Venetian morning. Such effects cannot be seen at any other time of day, so it is well worthwhile to be up early to just see the magical effects of Venice in the early morning.

Through and Beyond in Venice

Watercolour 13" x 19"

This scene, so typical of the quieter domestic areas of Venice, is seen from the Rio dei Sette Martiri. I was sketching with a few friends, all of whom had settled down within a stone's throw of each other but all tackling different subjects.

It was May 1999 and the problems in the former Yugoslavia were at their height. Many of the Venetians were not slow to make their views known with large banners draped from their balconies with such slogans as 'Clinton Killer' and 'Go home Brits'.

We all felt a deal of animosity towards us on that trip – at one point, as I was sitting by a house sketching, a beer bottle crashed to the ground at my feet from a window somewhere above me!

Another episode occurred as we were working just by where this painting was done. Norman, one of our party, was well into his painting seated by a wall, when out of an apartment came a lady with a basket of washing. Ignoring Norman she pegged out her smalls, both to the left and then well to the right of the artist. Casually observing this I was thinking how considerate it was of her. But no! She then took out of the basket a large sheet and hung it directly in front and within a foot of poor old Norman, totally obliterating his view. A few minutes after, he appeared from behind the sheet like an actor from the wings, with the prophetic words "I reckon she did that on purpose, don't you?"

One couldn't help but see the funny side of such a situation and of course we have never let Norman forget it. But despite two or three more incidents that year we still enjoyed our visit, but felt after the first day or two that it might be wiser for a while to avoid certain areas of the city which the Venetians quite rightly regard as rather more their own.

WESTON.

The Coffee Urn, Venice
Watercolour 10.5" x 8"

This is the interior of the popular little café in the Campo Santa Margharita. My painting on page 108 illustrates its modest façcade. Inside however is a real treat for those who like a touch of the Art Deco style. A coloured glass ceiling looks down on to white walls with etched mirrors in what is a small and intimate interior dominated by the most magnificent coffee urn in all Venice.

Its polished brass and copper gurgles and sighs with a hint of steam that is reminiscent of another age. The young man in charge tweaks and cajoles its levers and valves into providing whatever is demanded of it: espresso, cappuccino, or whatever else. Cups are kept warm under the dome at the top which is surmounted by a supreme crested eagle in fine style.

I liked the marble-topped counter too, on which it stands, with its dark mahogany and carved frieze, a fitting base for such a majestic machine!

Venice is a city full of surprises and this is only one of them. I just had to paint it of course and what fun it was – another example of the unusual things that have excited me in this most exciting of cities.

Gondola Workshop, Venice
Watercolour 10" x 16"

This interior is set within one of the ramshackle old sheds where gondolas have been built at the Campo San Trevaso for centuries. I have been privileged to be able to work within the complex there many times – it is such a fascinating place.

There are very few gondola yards left in Venice and the squero, which means boat-yard, at San Trovaso, has great character. Its wooden buildings have an Alpine look to them, most unusual for Venice, and in total contrast to the surrounding architecture.

A sketchbook can be a passport to many places where the public would not normally go and these workshops were just one. Obviously one must not get in the way of anyone doing their work, but to be able to actually observe at close quarters how gondolas are built and to watch the many age-old traditions of craftsmanship that go into them is a privilege and helps in painting them convincingly.

This almost monochromatic composition shows a gondola at a half-built stage, surrounded by the clutter of workshop paraphernalia and equipment. Drawing plays a big part in this painting which was done with only three colours – raw sienna, vandyke brown and neutral tint.

Corner Shop, Venice
Watercolour 9" x 13"

This is one of those off-beat subjects I delight in painting. It is really all about textures and colour, those delicious blues contrasting with the straw colour of the fruit boxes and the whites and golds on the walls.

Those walls, with their chipped and rugged textures, somehow complement the textures of the light wood of the boxes with their broken and irregular slats. Just recently I returned to see this shop again with a friend who owns this painting, only to find it is now a fashion boutique.

Venice is full of small shops, some where it is difficult to make out just what they sell. There is a dusty, cobwebbed window in the Via Garibaldi showing a model boat and a couple of ancient woodworking tools, but I can't for the life of me guess what is for sale inside - it might be plumbers' equipment but I am not sure!

Another lovely surprise is the old chemist's shop on the Strada Nuova, absolutely complete with its original and beautiful mahogany furniture and ceramics. It is now next to a modern pharmacy but has been kept as ever it was.

Fruit shops and stalls abound everywhere and so often make lovely subjects to paint. It is not only the colour of the fruits that is so appealing but so often their boxes sport colourful labels, as here in this painting, so typical of dozens of corner shops in the city.

Jazz in
Campo Santa Margherita, Venice
Watercolour 12" x 20"

We had been for a meal and an evening cruise on the Grand Canal and came across this quartet with their female singer outside this little café in the Campo Santa Margherita. Fortunately I had my camera with me and chanced a few shots, then scribbled a quick drawing on a piece of paper. Sketchbooks should never be left in hotels!

Back home some time later this watercolour was the result. This café is one of my favourite places for a coffee and a rest between sketches when working in this area. Santa Margherita is one of the loveliest of Venice's open spaces.

By night as the painting indicates, it has a great atmosphere with many outdoor restaurants and so often some sort of entertainment. By day its fish and fruit stalls bring the locals to mingle with the visitors and to sit in the sun simply to enjoy its relaxed and truly Italian atmosphere. It is a great place too for people watching.

As I sat sketching, an elderly lady with her poodle appeared. Elegantly attired, her dress and jewellery was straight out of 1930s Hollywood; the epitome of glamour and Art Deco style. One might have expected Humphrey Bogart to follow on. She disappeared into an anonymous doorway with a great flourish, just conscious I think that I was observing her so closely.

It is here too that Loris Marazzi carves his wonderful trompe l'oeil clothing from pine culled from the forests high in the Dolomites. His little studio in a corner of the Campo displays jackets and hats, handbags and shoes, which at first glance deceive the eye until the realisation that everything is carved from wood sinks in.

The Campo is always a buzz of activity, one day I had a long and complicated conversation with a local who watched me work intently for the best part of an hour. His smattering of English made concentration on drawing difficult, but when it was finished he declared ecstatically "It eassa the most beautiful picture I have never seena!"

Just then, however, a pigeon flying overhead let its thoughts on my sketch known in no uncertain terms right in the middle of the page. My new-found friend did a sort of demented little dance but whipped out a red handkerchief and swooped on the blessed drawing with vigour to erase the mess, but I am afraid the evidence remains to this day on that page of the sketchbook.

The delights and hazards of sketching in Venice!

Evening at Florians, Venice

Watercolour 14" x 20"

One of the great joys of Venice for ourselves and our friends is to sit in the Piazza di San Marco after supper to enjoy a coffee and maybe a brandy with that wonderful view of the Duomo floodlit whilst listening to the orchestra at the café Florian.

For over two hundred years Florians has been at the heart of Venice's cultural and artistic life where the great and the good have met to savour the atmosphere of this famous place and enjoy the intimacy of its unique painted and mirrored salons. I love the antiquity of Florians It first opened its doors in 1720 but was considerably refurbished in 1858 since when its decor has remained unchanged, despite the repeated flooding of the Piazza. On a severe flood the water sweeps through. It has caused the beautiful floors to be taken up and relaid a number of times.

Each small salon in the café Florian reflects in its faded grandeur a different aspect and atmosphere, from the room of Seasons or the Chinese room to the Oriental room and the Senate, and so on. Each is an intimate space of painted panels, gilded decoration and etched glass, softly lit by delicate globes held by bronze cherubs on carved columns.

It is all an outstanding example of Victorian and Venetian splendour, hailed at the time of the 1858 refurbishment as a 'triumph of good taste'. Perhaps not everyone would see it so, but as an unspoilt but gently decaying nineteenth century Venetian interior it possesses great atmosphere that is loved by many and certainly draws me back time after time.

Outside in the sunshine or under a night sky the waiters bustle to and fro, their silver trays held shoulder high whilst the orchestra entertains us with Debussy or Strauss.

I have tried to catch something of that in this painting, the musicians lit under their canopy and beyond, in the arcade, the entrance to the café Florian itself glittering under its many chandeliers and reflecting glass.

Concerto di Venezia
Watercolour 14" x 20"

These fragments of posters on a wall in Venice speak of music and the arts. I loved the main one with its mandolin and violin, set against an open book. It demanded to be painted faithfully, so much so that viewers of the painting have sometimes mistaken that section of it for collage work.

I was able to be more free on the rest of the picture and I thought the grafitti blended in well with the torn posters. Only a few years ago there was no grafitti on the walls in the city. Not so now, unfortunately, and some beautiful architecture is ruined by these vandals – their messages are it seems mostly of a political nature.

Through an Arch in the Market
Oil Painting 16" x 12"

San Georgio Maggiore, Venice
Watercolour 14" x 20"

The island of San Georgio Maggiore stands just off Venice in the lagoon and this view of the church with its splendid Palladian façade makes a fine and interesting focal point as seen here from the entrance to the Grand Canal.

To the right is the Dogana di Mare of 1676, the old customs house with the statue of Fortune standing on a globe of the world, forming the weathercock.

I wanted to create a breezy feel in this picture with a sky of scattered light cloud to give a feeling of space and movement with an oily reflection in the waters of the Grand Canal.

Early Morning, San Marco
Watercolour 13" x 19"

One has to be about well before breakfast to see the Piazza di San Marco so empty of people. Apart from the odd Venetian going to their work the street sweepers are perhaps the most prominent as they go about their seemingly unending task.

It is a lovely time of day to be there and one of the few when there is an unimpaired view of the architecture. The sun of course at so early an hour has not risen over the Duomo so both that and the Doges Palace, seen here on the right, are basically cool in colour as they reflect their arches in the marble floor of the Piazza.

In the foreground is one of the two enormous columns that mark the entrance to the Piazza from the Lagoon. It is a totally different picture to the one on page 92 seen from the Lagoon in the evening light when a westering sun catches the same buildings in a beautiful warm glow.

September Sunset, Venice
Watercolour 13" x 20"

The superb silhouette of the Della Salute at the entrance to the Grand Canal forms the focal point for this atmospheric painting at sunset. Seen across the lagoon from the Riva S Biagio it made an impressive and memorable sight that I could never forget. Venice in the early morning or as here in an evening light produces its most evocative and ethereal effects.

BERGEN and THE FJORDS

Our journeyings abroad have taken us only once to the Norwegian Fjords. We stayed for a part of our time in the enormous expanses of Sognefjord which in turn led us to the narrower and more dramatic enclosures of Naeroyfjord and Aurlandsfjord. I found these Fjords inspiring, particularly in more stormy weather when the steep cliff sides of the mountains seemed ever higher and more threatening, dwarfing any boat that ventured through at such a time.

From Aurlandsfjord a trip on the Flam rack railway is a must for the visitor to these parts. One does not have to be a railway enthusiast to enjoy the steep and winding journey ever upwards through some really spectacular mountain scenery and its amazing waterfalls. I have included a painting here of the lower reaches of the Flam Valley (page 119) where the river widens out on its journey down to Aurlandsfjord.

Contrasting with the green and grey scenery of the Fjords is the colour to be found in the lap-boarded architecture of both villages and towns. This is apparent, nowhere moreso perhaps, than in the city of Bergen where the steep streets that rise up from the harbourfront display houses painted in many pastel shades, and of course the inevitable white. Old Bergen is lovely and well worth the climb to experience the variety and detail of those lap-boarded structures with their neat and essentially tidy gardens.

Down by the harbour is the Bryggen, a collection of Bergen's oldest buildings, less colourful but nonetheless fascinating in its warped and ancient timbers and still reflecting many aspects of the commercial life of a city which depended for its prosperity on its harbour and the sea. To wander and of course sketch within the complex of those tottering old buildings was a great delight. I particularly liked the wooden-planked floorboards, open here and there to the sky, and lovely after a shower when figures became reflected in them.

These few Norwegian paintings will contrast considerably with the work done in France and Italy where a hot sun has its lasting effect on both general colour and the bleaching out on architecture. Norway is more likely to show a pallet of colours in the landscape akin to our own, with the earthy shades of umbers and ochres and warmer greens predominating.

The Mountains in Naeroyfjorden
Watercolour 8.5" x 13.5"

Interior in Ofredal
Oil Painting 12" x 10"

**Light and Shade in
Upper Bergen**
Watercolour 10" x 8.5"

Sunshine in Flamsdalen, Norway
Watercolour 13" x 10"

A trip on the spectacular railway line from Flam at the top of Aurlandsfjord is an exciting train journey that twists and turns on its steep climb along precipitous mountain sides to Myrdal, a journey of some twenty kilometres.

The line passes through no less than twenty tunnels between which can be seen some of the most wild and beautiful mountain scenery to be found anywhere in Norway. With some friends we took the train up to the mountain station at Myrdal and then back down again, changing sides in the carriage so as not to miss anything of the magnificent views. From the windows we saw walkers following the route along the valley bottom and I wished there had been time to explore more of this area on foot and with my sketchbook.

My painting here shows the Flam valley where one of the many great waterfalls cascade down the mountain sides to the river below. It is a complicated subject in terms of landscape painting but once again I have endeavoured to keep it as simple as possible with no fussy detail at all.

In the Bryggen, Bergen, Norway

Watercolour 8.5 x 12"

Bergen is an enjoyable and fascinating town where the old has been preserved alongside the new. The streets are teeming with well-cared-for clapboard houses painted in the Norwegian tradition of either bright colours or white.

On the harbour front is the Bryggen, a collection of some of the oldest houses and workplaces that have survived in Bergen. These wooden buildings reflect the fact that the sea fostered this place, for here are the quarters of mariners and merchants of the past.

Rope and sail makers and shipwrights once haunted the wooden-boarded alleyways of the Bryggen which still with its unique architecture reminds the visitor of the work that once was a part of everyday life on the waterfront.

This is certainly no museum. The alleyways today contain small shops but they have not been allowed to intrude on the history that is inherent within the buildings' various levels.

My painting shows one of the entrances – the buildings warped with the years and the wet boarded floor reflecting the figures against a strong light. It was an enjoyable painting to produce and I wanted to catch something of the antiquity of this extraordinary part of old Bergen.

Boatsheds at Leikanger, Sognefjord, Norway
Watercolour 13" x 18.5"

The wide expanse of Sognefjord creates a great contrast to the usual imagined image of the Norwegian fjord, narrow and steep sided. Sognefjord is rather more like a Scottish loch with the mountains more distant and remote.

Here at Leikanger I came across these interesting old boatsheds with their precarious stagings dipping into the water. The two children fishing gave a focal point and balance to the composition together with the snow-capped mountain beyond. There were some lovely fresh greens in the landscape which lightly reflected in the water and made a wonderful contrast to all those warm colours in both the sky and the buildings.

Dramatic Light, Naeroyfjorden, Norway
Watercolour 12″ x 16.5″

The steep-sided Norwegian fjords can be very beautiful and on a sunny day with still reflections in the water they do indeed present a picture-book image. But on a day of dark cloud or breaking mist the closeness of the mountain sides seem oppressive and dangerous with that brooding atmosphere that so inspires me to paint.

In this fairly large watercolour, done at full strength, I wanted to evoke that feeling of the hills closing in, almost claustrophobic – the low cloud breaking the steep cliffs to add mystery to the further reaches of the fjord.

The boat, far distant, presents an idea of the scale of those mountains and the narrow confines of Naeroyfjorden. The challenge with using watercolour at its limits strength-wise as in this painting, is to keep it fresh. There is little room for error and here a good ninety-five percent has been done with only one wash application, keeping the brushwork lively and avoiding any overworking with secondary washes.

ITHACA

To reach Ithaca one must first fly to the island of Cephallonia. From there a boat ferries visitors across the sea – a journey of some fourteen miles, and after the barren volcanic landscape of Cephallonia, Ithaca shows itself as a verdant island, small by comparison, but very beautiful and equally historic. Homer's epic poems have made its name known throughout the world.

Kioni is, I think, the loveliest place on the island. It is entered from the Ionian sea through lush green hills, its harbour guarded over on the one side by the ruins of three windmills and on the other by the red-roofed whitewashed houses on the tiny harbour front

The last time Mary and I set foot on Ithaca's soil was in 1990. Tourism then had still not taken off to any great extent – there were only two small tavernas in Kioni and a visit to one of those was not to be encouraged! No doubt things have altered since, but I hope Kioni's harbour frontage has not suffered too much from development through greater tourism over the years. The view of it in the painting on page 124 is from where we stayed on our first visit in 1989, and made a lovely composition that leads the eye down to the harbour beyond.

Although most of these paintings in this section on Ithaca were done shortly after our visits there I still occasionally look out the sketchbooks from those years and produce paintings from them, and this one, 'Down to the Harbour Kioni', is one of those done more recently in 2006. And there is still more inspiring material to use in the future. I think it was the colour I saw in Ithaca that so excited me; those dramatic contrasts of hot and cool colours, and the deep strength of shaded areas and cast shadows, so much of it set against the transparent turquoise waters of the Ionian Sea.

**Down to the Harbour,
Kioni, Ithaca**

Watercolour 17" x 11"

In the Monastery of Kathara, Ithaca
Acrylic 12.5" x 9"

The Mayor of Kioni also ran the local taxi service. He drove Mary and I high into the hills, at times a hair raising journey, to this lonely and deserted Monastery at Kathara.

We had arranged for a return journey with him for later in the afternoon, but I admit to us both feeling a trifle abandoned as his car sped off in a cloud of dust with only a faint hope that he had understood our request!

However, the silence and stillness of this lovely place soon made us forget our concerns about the possible fifteen mile walk back as we entered the cool sanctuary of what was a captivating interior where time had literally stood still.

The doorway in the painting led through into an inner courtyard where our voices almost echoed in the silence of that place. But we were soon to discover that we were not quite alone, for out of an ancient door came a rather bent old lady who looked after the goats we had seen outside. She obviously took a pride in keeping the courtyard clean and the abundance of plants therein well watered. She plied us with hot black coffee, a welcoming gesture we appreciated, but then left us to soak in the atmosphere of this hidden gem. There was an amazing sense of peace in that place which we will never forget and the hours we spent just sitting there were sheer bliss.

I did a couple of drawings, and the accompanying picture of the courtyard was the result some time afterwards.

By mid-afternoon we started to walk towards Kioni and were greatly relieved to see a distant cloud of dust miraculously turn into our promised taxi. The Mayor had not let us down!

The Courtyard, Kathara
Watercolour 14" x 14"

The Bells of Rachi, Ithaca
Watercolour 8" x 9"

This gorgeous pair of bells made an intriguing subject. The smaller one, rich in colour against the blue of the sky and the larger bell with its detail and cast shadows, made for a composition that stepped down nicely from the right.

Every so often I will come across a detail on a building or some small part of it, that makes a picture and says as much (if not more) than a painting of the whole thing.

Sunshine After Rain, Ithaca
Watercolour 13" x 9"

I remember I had this painting in an exhibition in my gallery here at the Lazy Acre shortly after our return from Ithaca in 1990. It attracted the attention of a Yorkshire woman who had visited in previous years and whom I knew to be a farmer's wife. "I do like them hens", she said, "I've a mind to take it for him. He couldn't come this year – too much on". I replied that I thought it was the sort of painting he would like, whereupon she peered once again at the price and said "Ah, go on then, I'll have it for him, will you take a cheque?"

That said, she promptly wrote out the cheque but just before signing it she asked where the picture was done? I should of course have said Yorkshire, it could well have been after all, but no, I said it was done from my trip to Ithaca.

She stared hard at the painting and then said "What, you mean they are Greek hens?" "Well, yes", I replied. "Oh well I don't want it then. He wouldn't want Greek hens". With that the cheque book was slammed firmly closed and buried in her enormous handbag, and I had lost a sale.

However, I retrieved things a little later in the show when another couple were showing interest in the same painting. I told them what had happened previously. They thought it was so funny that they bought the picture on the strength of it! I have been cautious about Greek hens ever since.

The Church at Rachi
Watercolour 13" x 9"

High above the harbour of Kioni, on Ithaca, is Rachi — considered to be a part of Kioni, but separated by a road that straggles up the hillside to culminate in a dozen or so houses and the inevitable church.

Another day of hot sun found me once again seeking the shadow of either trees or buildings and here in this yard, behind a soundly shuttered house, was this super subject. As I approached a large and disreputable dozing dog opened one eye and growled a menacing, if half-hearted warning. But I stood my ground and sat down on a handy wooden box in the shade of the house wall. Fortunately the soft old dog decided that I must be too knackered by the heat to do any harm and so came across and lay down full length over my feet, heaving a sigh of deep resignation.

I did this large watercolour afterwards in the studio and have kept it at home, it is so much a part of our memories of Ithaca.

And the dog! He slept and snored the whole time that I was sketching, but seemed to sense when I was about to finish for he shook himself down and returned to the shaded spot where I had first seen him, to continue his lunchtime slumbers.

He was not so daft. As Noel Coward would have it, only mad dogs and Englishmen go out in the mid-day sun!

Fishing Boats at Polis Bay, Ithaca

Acrylic 9" x 11"

This wonderful old fishing boat made an irresistible and colourful subject. I loved the amount of clutter within the boat and the canopy over the top. The blue of the water cast reflected lights on to the side of the boat giving lots of broken colour effects.

The second boat in the background added nicely to the composition and had a different but equally characterful appearance.

Upland Farm, Kioni
Watercolour 9" x 20"

IRELAND

I first set foot on Irish soil during the 1970s when I was commissioned to do some work in County Armargh. It was not a good time to be there with the troubles in the North as they were, and although the commission was based close to Belfast my journeying frequently took me across the border into Donegal and Co. Sligo.

The constant element of danger at that time very quickly heightened my perception of what life was like every day in that area. As a well-intentioned policeman told me in no uncertain terms on my arrival at my client's house, "If you go out in that cap, from a hundred yards its a black beret, you'll go back in a box". The need to be constantly on one's guard, especially when standing for some time in an exposed spot sketching was paramount to avoiding any likelihood of the constable's prophecy bearing fruit!

This small group of Irish paintings reproduced here however represent a very different time and face of the country and are all from a trip made with friends to Co. Galway in 2001. The only thing to avoid then was the very changeable weather, the worst of which was encountered on a trip by boat to the Island of Inishbofin, just off the Conemara coastline.

We had made the mistake of buying our tickets from the wrong shop of the two available in Cleggan, so instead of the comfortable passenger boat to make the journey we were directed towards the local mail boat, a rusting old bucket of a tub with little in the way of comfort and a distinct air of chance that it might go anywhere.

The journey out, however, was fine with a following wind and a glimpse of sun, but once on Inishbofin's soil things took a decided turn for the worse as a soft Irish morning gradually worked its way up into a lashing, drenching and relentless downpour that knew absolutely no mercy, and we were stuck there until the wretched mail boat returned at 5.30pm. But the indignity did not end there as we returned to the quay to find that the very comfortable-looking passenger boat had returned and was ready to sail with its tea-sipping passengers smiling out at the sodden wretches who were abandoned on that rain-lashed quayside and condemned to the rigours of the go-as-they-pleased nature of the mail boat.

One could never forget that journey back as we sat soaked to the skin on hard wooden benches with steam slowly rising from all aboard including a blessed dog that had somehow lain itself across our feet, its doleful eyes pleading adoption and equally desperate not to spend another day of its life on Inishbofin! That said there were some heartily good days and times spent on that trip to Co. Galway which perhaps these paintings will represent. Fourteen sketches were produced and probably as many paintings from them since, amongst which were two from the Inishbofin day, one reproduced here.

Perhaps I have written enough to introduce this section and give a flavour of this lovely part of the world, so as the Irish would have it, "I'll take a five minute break for ten minutes and come back in half an hour!"

Cottage at Ballyconneely
Watercolour 8.5" x 13.5"

Low Tide at Leenaon, Co. Galway
Watercolour 8.5" x 13.5"

Cottages at Cleggan
Watercolour 7" x 11"

Sunlight at Aasleagh Falls
Watercolour 7.5" x 12"

Desolation on Inishbofin
Watercolour 12" x 19"

A pile of lobster pots and a derelict cottage said a lot about this little Irish island off the Connemara coastline.

I wanted this picture to express the desolation and sparseness of the landscape and a loneliness which I feel the stationary figure and the upturned wheelbarrow somehow help to create. It is a painting that when I first did it I was not sure that I liked, but it was what I meant. Now that I have lived with it for a while I do like it and regard it as one of my best Irish pictures, both for its content and for its overall effect.

Early Light on the Estuary
Watercolour 7.5" x 19"

We were staying on the harbour front at Clifden in Co. Galway and this view presented itself from our window. The town dropped down to the water on a morning of soft weather, but brightening.

It is a picture of many subtle shades of green and greys: warm mauve-greys to cool blue ones and very delicate mixes of soft greens that here and there just reflected in the estuary.

It demanded a simple clean wash treatment to portray the nature and atmosphere of the scene.

The Steamer at Barnaderg Bay
Watercolour 13.5" x 20.5"

This old tub had such character and textures that it would have been difficult to ignore it as the subject for a large watercolour. I doubt it had moved far for a long time and even the quayside was overgrown with a disused air about it that added to the atmosphere of the whole scene.

The rust was great fun to paint, much speckling with the splatter from a flat brush, and those delicious deep warm shades of Indian and light red that changed to a deep blue nearer the water level. The sky is very much as on the day I was there – very Irish!

SCOTLAND

Until more recently it had been some years since I last painted in Scotland, but a stay on the Applecross Peninsula in Wester Ross way above the Kyle of Lochalsh brought home to me just how much I have been missing.

During the 1970s, early in my professional career, I was commissioned by Sir Robert McAlpine & Sons to paint a considerable number of pictures for them of their various projects. Subjects ranged from the building of nuclear power stations along the Clyde at Hunterston and Inverkip, to the construction of concrete oil rigs across the water on Dunoon.

Further work took me to Edinburgh where I painted their activities on the building of a huge shopping complex. But they were not all industrial subjects and more commissions saw me working in Perthshire at Loch Katrine and west towards Fort William. Many pictures resulted from those times spent in the Highlands. Mostly oils, I have particular memories of paintings done in Glen Coe, Loch Leven and Loch Lochy. I have no idea where they are now!

My more recent discovery of the wild nature of Wester Ross, with its coastal views across to the Isle of Skye and, by contrast, its formidable mountain ranges surrounding Loch Torridon, has held me totally spellbound. It has a wild and ragged beauty that varies from the dramatic grandeur of its high peaks under broken cloud to the light-filled vistas over a winding and dipping landscape along the waters of the inner sound.

I hope the paintings of this area will express my enthusiasm and inspiration better than these few words and show something of the essence of the Scottish landscape as I have found it.

'The Spirit of Scotland'
Oil Painting 24" x 36"

At some time during the spring of 1993 Mary and I were invited to a cocktail party aboard the sailing vessel *Spirit of Scotland*. She was berthed in St Katherine's Dock, just below Tower Bridge on the Thames, and made a very splendid sight for the occasion.

This painting came out of that evening and was presented to Scottish Nuclear who had organised the event to make interested parties aware of the work they sponsored to provide training and adventure at sea for disadvantaged youngsters.

Over the Forth
Oil Painting 30" x 40"

I painted this dramatic image of the Forth Bridge in 1974, and for a while it hung in the London office of The Hon. Sir William McAlpine before he rehung it at his home.

The sheer majesty and size of the structure dwarfing the houses and wet roofs below was something I really wanted to portray. The contrast between the bridge and the locomotive with its train passing over it also emphasises its enormous scale. The engine, appropriately, is the ever famous 'Flying Scotsman'.

Deserted Croft at Callakille

Watercolour 94" x 13"

Ruined and deserted homesteads are a common sight along the wilder reaches of Wester-Ross and here at Callakille there are several clustered together in a sad reminder of life in days past.

I liked the rusty corrugated iron roof on this little place with its bright orange colour that sang out against the light on the water, and the feeling the whole composition gave of desolation and abandonment.

It would be impossible to linger in this place without wondering about the families who once eked out a living in the harshness of this landscape and what happened to them when their livelihoods disappeared?

On the Road to Applecross
Watercolour 12.5" x 19"

The road between Loch Torridon and Applecross is constantly surprising, varying from steep mountain bends with dangerous drops to the coastal stretches along the Inner Sound where its moorland areas pitch it constantly up and down as it winds its way along the coast.

In the distance is the Isle of Skye, seen here in an afternoon light. The road disappeared into deep hollows and reappeared again to wind its way towards the deserted homes of Callakille, visible in the middle distance.

I enjoyed constructing this painting with its challenge to create the feeling of such a vast landscape.

Approaching Storm, Loch Torridon
Watercolour 8" x 13"

The brilliant light on the water gave a dramatic contrast with the foreground and offset the effects of the distant storm-clouds across the loch.

The little red-roofed cottage, a familiar sight to anyone who travels that road, made the perfect focal point for this dramatic and atmospheric view of Loch Torridon.

Fishing Sheds near Applecross
Watercolour 9" x 12.5"

Old Boat at Kenmore
Watercolour 6" x 11.5"

The View from a Place Called Sand
Watercolour 9″ x 21″

Loch Torridon
Watercolour 9.5" x 13.5"

Snow on Loch Leven

Oil Painting 12" x 16"

This is a recent painting done from one of my sketches from the 1970s. My memory of the scene is quite vivid and the snow on the tops made for a lasting impression in my mind It is a painting that relies for its appeal to a large extent on the contrast between the greater part of warm colour with the icy blue cold areas of the mountains.

Light on the Rocks, Lonbain
Watercolour 9" x 13.5"

A strong morning light lit this scene on the Applecross peninsula. As it happens, the view was from the windows of our breakfast room and consequently the urgency to record it somewhat delayed the process of getting the first meal of the day over with at its normal pace!

Such light only lasts for a short time and constantly alters so one needs to be quick with a sketch or camera to catch it.

In painting this scene later in the studio I have tried to create a sense of moving light and shadow combined with strong colour.

Deserted Community, Callekille
Watercolour 7" x 21"

HOME AGAIN

As the title to this final section suggests, we are back again in England with a further selection of pictures from some widely varying locations.

Once again my passion for the railways, their architecture, and steam engines shows through to contrast with subjects like the 'Devon Pulpit' (page 160) found in a corner of the church in the delightfully unspoilt little town of Bampton, and also from the same county my painting of 'Sea Mist at Hope Cove' (page 155).

I set out at the beginning of this book to make it as full of contrasts as my work would allow, and I hope that has proved to be so, from the sun and hot colour of the Mediterranean countries to the softer atmosphere of our own shores.

As I write this now we are in the middle of another English winter and memories of those long hot days under a Continental sun seem a million miles away. But today as I walked down the village towards the church the sun

Winter work in Devon.

broke through the early morning fog to make delicate and magical effects of light. The bare winter trees were softened in the receding mist and the church was lit by a gentle light that brought out the warmth and beauty of its crumbling stone.

Close by, the nearest cottage also caught that same ethereal light. It is a light that I have always found to be inspiring, albeit not the easiest of effects to paint despite its apparent simplicity! However, on my return to the studio I just had to have a go and the result now concludes the sequence of paintings in this book (page 168).

It is, I suppose, a very gentle picture, but one that I feel is essentially English in both its subject and treatment, and in some small way pays homage to those nineteenth-century practitioners of the art of watercolour painting whose work remains at the roots of English painting and is a constant inspiration to all like myself who follow in their wake.

Heavy Freight for Tyne Dock
Watercolour 12" x 15"

A British Railways' Class 9 Freight locomotive works hard, throwing a huge plume of black smoke skywards in the effort to pull its endless train of wagons. This is an atmospheric watercolour done on a damp paper to capture the sense of movement in the train and the damp atmosphere of the surrounding countryside.

Sea Mist at Hope Cove
Watercolour 12.5" x 20.5"

A simple subject that is pure atmosphere. We had been out all day in brilliant sunshine and returned to our hotel in this lovely part of Devon to find our view of the little bay of Hope Cove intermittently obscured by mist. But as the sun broke through some lovely effects of light filled the view wih a magic that was an absolute joy to watch.

Studio painting followed soon afterwards and this is one I have not fallen out with!

The Seat in the Weeds
Watercolour 9.5" x 12.5"

An evening visit with my local sketch club to a wildflower farm in Nottinghamshire proved to be surprisingly fruitful for subjects to paint. This old rusting cast-iron seat, quite overgrown, presented itself against a background of ox-eye daisies and filtered sunlight which just caught it here and there to create some delicious deep shadows in contrast to the whites of the daisies and the pale green of the undergrowth.

It would be easy to get bogged down in detail with a subject like this but I have tried to avoid excessive detail by the use of good broad areas of colour.

Breakfast at Rempstone
Watercolour 13" x 17"

With the engines ready for the show, cleaned, polished and steamed up, I caught this little group having breakfast under their sunshade beside their showman's caravan and could not resist the subject for a large watercolour.

I have kept the whole scene as loosely treated as I could with consideration to the detail involved in such engines. But strong darks and a suggestion of shapes rather than drawn detail worked well and lets the engines blend into the free brushwork of the setting.

Waiting
Watercolour 13" x 17.5"

A hot afternoon sun at a quiet station somewhere in Devon, well Buckfastleigh actually, although the location does not really matter. It could be anywhere on an English country branch line although the landscape is of course distinctly Devonian.

The porters and a lone passenger seek the sanctuary of the shade to escape the heat, and grass grows between the tracks. Somewhere far distant a faint whistle is heard to reassure the world that the next arrival will in fact appear to liven things up for a short while.

It was that stillness and quiet of the hot afternoon in Devon that I wanted to come across in this painting so I chose to use simple wash work with only the minimal amount of detail to tell the story. A looseness of line, nothing too precise, and careful attention to the relative tone values was the key to creating that 'lazy afternoon' feel in this particular picture.

The Mariner's Cottage
Watercolour 10" x 13"

Here at Burnham Overy Town on a turn of the road sits this tiny cottage with the most extraordinary frontage. The faded lettering over the door, now almost indecipherable, once boldly announced the name of its owner, and his profession of Mariner, which survives enough to be clearly readable. Not that such is entirely necessary perhaps with those stone figures like ships' figureheads either side of the door.

Such a splendid display on such a humble cottage. Who was this mariner who would go to such lengths to announce to the world just where he lived? It is intriguing and I would like to know more.

The two further heads backed on flat stone, that stand either side of where a gate would have been are now rather neglected and weed-grown but add to the curiosity of this place which stands just over a mile away from the sea.

It made an intriguing subject to paint where the emphasis is on textures and the feeling of neglect and faded glory.

A Devon Pulpit

Watercolour 11.5" x 7.5"

I do like church interiors, not so much the grand views as these intimate little corners where so often light plays a major part in the conception of the painting.

Here the light hit the creamy wall behind the pulpit and highlighted the Victorian oil lamp on its ornate brass support. The pulpit itself was almost totally in silhouette save for those telling highlights on its face. The church, by the way, is the delightful little church at Bampton in Devon which has provided me with one or two subjects worth painting.

The Glory of Ely
Watercolour 11" x 17.5"

What a magnificent sight the Cathedral at Ely makes, sitting as it does in the flat landscape of the Cambridgeshire fens. Seen across the fields it towers above the city in all its splendour whether it be in sunlight or as in this painting, on a day of silvery light which caught the roofs still wet after a brief shower.

There are many subtle shades of grey and green in this picture with the whole landscape being treated as simply as possible – no detail at all – and even on the Cathedral I have only just suggested the shapes of windows so as not to spoil the silhouetted shape of the entire building. Simplicity was the keynote to capturing the atmosphere of the day and landscape.

Fish Sheds at Walberswick

Watercolour 9.5" x 12"

There are a number of these old sheds along the estuary at Walberswick, and even more on the other side at Southwold. They have a character that only time, use and neglect can bestow on such structures. This pair, with the light criss-crossing their frontages, make a statement about the fishing community that works out of Walberswick.

The nets with the blue and white boat complete the imagery. Any detail in this painting is kept to a little drawing, sometimes in ink, on the facias of the sheds and nets, etc. It gave me the opportunity to use very strong plain darks on the sides and under the sheds, the further one brown, the nearer black.

The threatening sky adds much to the atmosphere of the scene and the two figures with a dog gives scale and also the feeling that they ought to hurry on before the storm breaks.

The Vice
Watercolour 12″ x 8.5″

Blue Boat at Walberswick
Watercolour 11" x 17"

Boatshed in Salcombe
Watercolour 9.5" x 14"

'Britannia' at Crewe
Oil Painting 30" x 40"

Inside the Shed
Watercolour 12" x 18"

A Saturday morning spent drawing this subject at Loughborough on the Great Central Railway in Leicestershire proved to be well worthwhile when it came to producing this large watercolour later in the studio. Such close detail in watercolour is not easy to achieve and so the knowledge gained from observation through careful drawing on the spot is essential to approach such a subject with confidence.

The whole scene with the men, and the view out into the yard, combine to create a picture that could have been set at any time during the last years of steam traction on our railways – something not always possible on preserved lines - but the Great Central has it about right. I hope they never get to tidy it up!

Winter Sun, Kirby Bellars
Watercolour 10" x 9"